IF ZEBRAS ZIPLINED

By Mary Barry

© 2020 Mary Barry

All rights reserved. No portion of this book may be reproduced in any fashion, print, facsimile, digital or electronic, or by any method yet to be developed, without express permission by the copyright holder.

ISBN 978-1-7339955-4-2

For information, contact the author:

Mary Barry
email: atozebrabooks@gmail.com
website: www.atozebrabooks.com

Published by:

Chilidog Press LLC
pbronson@chilidogpress.com

Chilidog Press LLC
Loveland, Ohio
www.chilidogpress.com

Illustrated by Steve Wallace
Book Layout by Andy Melchers

IF ZEBRAS ZIPLINED

By Mary Barry

Illustrations by Steve Wallace

For Trisha, Christy, Lynn, Connie, Paula and, of course, Bob.

Mary Barry

For my eight grandkids, Carson, Stevin, Rowan, Landon, Avery, Owen, Burke and Josie. (Thank you, Terri.)

Steve Wallace

HOW MANY CAN YOU FIND?

Each page has things that start with its letter.
See how many you can find. The answers are
in the back of the book.

"Ah, ah, ah, Ayden!
Apple pie is not for now,
my little guy."

a a

Belle feeds her goldfish,
Buddy and Troubles.
"Blub-blub," they reply,
saying "Thank you" with bubbles.

**The campfire crackles,
sleeping bags unfold,
Cindy serves cocoa
and ghost stories are told.**

C c

"Duh-duh-duh-duh."
Dino dribbles the ball down the floor,
then shoots for the basket.
It's a *three-point score!!!*

D d

"Ehhhhhhhhhhhhh."
What's that
hum Ethan hears…
with his great big,
beautiful elephant ears?

"Flop, flop," goes the tire
on Fred's new dirt bike.
Uh-oh, it's a flat!
Do you know what that's like?

Grace says "Goo-goo,"
to George, her big brother.
Some day they'll be able
to talk to each other.

G g

"Hey, Hunter!" calls Haley.
"Come back and play."
"Ha-ha!" howls Hunter,
as he runs away.

Iguana Ike's scared of bugs.
How about you?
"Iiiiiiiiiiiiiiicky!" he yells,
as one jumps on his shoe.

"Ji-ji-ji," jiggles Jellyfish Jean.
"Let's have a party
and eat jellybeans!"

Kate's chopping wood,
"Crack-crack," whacks the axe.
While the blazing campfire,
krackles and cracks.

K k

"La-la-la," trills Lil,
singing her loveliest song.
Well, lovely until…
Lou and Lee sing along.

"Mmmmmmm, chocolate milk!"
Matthew says with a wink,
"A lip-smacking delight."
What's your favorite drink?

"Nnnnnnnn," hums the drone
as it swoops down low.
"Nnnnnnnnnnnnnn," it shoots up.
Noah shouts, "Way to go!"

N n

Ollie Oat loves the opera,
so his Dad says, "Let's go."
"We'll 'oo' and 'ah' at the opera
and really enjoy the show!"

Pete's boat putt-putts round and round.
He yells, "Me hearties, Heave ho!"
Pete sounds like a sea dog, barking,
"Thar she blows" and a "Yo-ho-ho."

"Quack-quack," quack the ducks.
They are great quacking snackers.
They love swimming and diving
and eating Quinn's crackers.

"Rrrrrrrrroar!!"
Rory, the rhino, roars really loud.
Because that's his job,
and the crowd is wowed.

"Sssssssss," says Sam,
the slithering snake.
Savannah Swan sees him
slide into the lake.

"Tick-tick, tick-tick,"
Tom hears the sound…
of time ticking by,
never more to be found.

Tt

"Uhhhhhhh???" wonders Uri.
Should he run for it? Or…
grab an umbrella
as he heads out the door?

"Vvvvvvvvvoom!"
Hear the sound of the vampire bees,
as they fly 'round the tulips
and the zombie trees.

"Wwwwwwwhoosh!"
Out go the candles on Wally's cake.
When it's your birthday,
what wish will you make?

Xylophones, x-rays, exercise, exits—
quite a collection of various Xs.

"Yackety-yawn!" yells the yellow yak
as he scratches his back...
and jumps in the sack.

Yy

"Zzzzzzzzzach!" shouts Zebra,
"Come out and play!
Let's zipline at the zoo today."

How Many Can You Find?

Letter	Number	List of objects to count
A	5	Alligators, Apron, Apple Pie, Airplane, Apple Tree
B	9	Bear, Bow, Boat, Bee, Bowl, Book, Bottle, Bunny, Bubbles
C	5	Camel, Cat, Camper, Cups of Cocoa, Campfire
D	4	Dinosaur, Dog, Donkey, Door
E	6	Elephants, Eagle, Eggs, Earth, Electric Shaver, Ears
F	5	Frogs, Fox, Fence, Flowers, Feet
G	8	Giraffes, Goat, Glasses, Game, Grasshopper, Grapes, Garbage Can, Grass
H	7	Hippos, Hat, Helicopter, Hula Hoop, House, Hummingbird, Hill
I	4	Iguana, Inchworm, Ice Cubes, Insect
J	8	Jellyfish, Jug, Jellybeans, Jewelry, Jar, Jacket, Jackknife, Jump Rope
K	5	Kangroos, Kitten, Kite, Key, Kettle
L	5	Ladybugs, Lily, Leaves, Lollipop, Lizard

M	6	Moose, Milk, Monkey, Mouse, Mountain, Moon
N	6	Newt, Nightcrawler, Nickle, Nuts, Necklace, Net
O	3	Octopuses, Orangutan, Ostrich
P	11	Pirate, Pig, Pirate Hat, Parrot, Pony, Penguin, Parachute, Plane, Pelican, Pond, (Eye) Patch
Q	4	Quail (named Quinn), Quilt, Quarter, Queen
R	10	Rhino, Rabbit, Reindeer, Racoon, Rat, Rocks, Rainbow, Rattlesnake, Rudolph, Red Nose
S	10	Swan, Snake, Shoe, Squirrel, Skunk, Sheep, Sailboat, Sun, Sunflowers, Snapping Turtle
T	5	Turtle, Tomatoes, Todd the Toad, Tree, Toadstools
U	5	Unicorn, Umbrella, Unicycle, Up (Arrow), Urn
V	5	Vampire Bees, Vulture, Violin, Volcano, Vine
W	5	Walrus, Whale, Waterfall, Watermelon, Water
X	2	Xylophone, X-ray
Y	2	Yak, Yacht
Z	4	Zebra, Zipper, Zipline, Zoo

If you find more things in the pictures that start with that letter, contact Mary at: atozebrabooks@gmail.com

About the author:
Mary Barry is a Registered Nurse, mother of four, grandmother of nine and great-grandmother of one. The concept of *If Zebras Ziplined* began when Mary helped her girls learn to read. She shared the book with family, friends and teachers who used it with great success. Two of her nieces loved the book so much and read it so often that they memorized it! Mary's dream is to help new readers learn phonics more easily. So this book, the first of her *A To Zebra Series*, is a dream come true. Mary lives in Cincinnati, Ohio. She recently lost her dear husband, Bob, to dementia. In honor of his valiant battle with this disease, Mary will donate a portion of the earnings from *If Zebras Ziplined* to the Alzheimer's Association.

About the illustrator:
Steve Wallace, AKA "Grandude," is a retired architect. Steve always wanted to be a cartoonist, and with the completion of his third book of illustrations the dream is closer. Steve now lives in his hometown of Milford, Ohio with his wife, where they enjoy golf and time with their five kids and eight grandkids.

Made in the USA
Monee, IL
25 July 2021